ORANGE TASTE

Ndukwo Kalu Ugah

ORANGE TASTE

(a collection of poems)

NDUKWO KALU UGAH

Ndukwo Kalu Ugah

Copyright ©2016 NDUKWO KALU UGAH

ISBN: 978-978-956-861-1

All rights reserved.
No part of this book may be reproduced, distributed, stored in a retrieval system or transmitted, in any form or by any means, electronic, electrostatic, magnetic tape, mechanical, photocopying, recording or otherwise without prior written permission from the Publisher.
For information about permission to reproduce selections from this book, write to info@wrr.ng
National Library of Nigeria Cataloguing-in-Publication Data

Printed and Published in Nigeria by:

Words Rhymes & Rhythm Limited
Suite C309, Global Plaza Plot 366, Obafemi Awolowo Way,
Jabi District, Abuja, Nigeria.
08169027757, 08060109295

www.wrr.ng

Orange Taste

CONTENTS

DEDICATION 7
ACKNOWLEDGEMENT 8
COMMENTS...9
Pictures in the frames 12
Strangers..13
London Bridge...14
The Prisons..15
Rats 16
Freedom Throes..17
How we became friends 18
Love Me 19
Flies..20
Let me cry 21
Son, Father and Mother 22
Father Around..23
Sad Corner 24
Drag me not again.....................................25
Better the world...26
The crown of life..27
I Can't Stay 28
Rain In May 29
Save a mother 30
Together a country 31
Streams of Love 32
Brain Washed 33
What if we all went blind?.........................34
A still place in the market 36

Your life is in dust 37
Black Ant 38
Hail O Biafra 40
Without The Blacks 41
On The Feast Day 42
Who Dies Next? 43
In all these, I thank God 44
Confined by the Night 45
Negroes 46
St. Peters' Church 47
Together Apart 48
Our Quest 49
African Grasses 50
Tamer of all 51
Shall I live or die? 53
A boy of peace 54
Public Funds 55
A poet's mind 57
Mother-In law 58
My Child 59
Father 60
A trip in *gwongworo* 61
Let's call back 62
An Igbo 63
Come back brother 64
Scriptures must be fulfilled 66
The tree of life 67
The craftsman 68

Orange Taste

A walk in alcohol 69
War danced 70
Child Loss 71
Wedding day 72
Okomba 73
Chinua Achebe 75
Mosquitoes 76
The Youth 77
The new God 78
They clap death 79
Ojukwu 80
Tragedienne 81
Orange taste 82

DEDICATION

To a brother (Mr. Michael Obewu-Kupex)
Who encouraged me to read even newspapers
And God Almighty
That gave me feathers.

ACKNOWLEDGEMENT

First, to my beloved siblings: Eme, Onuoha, Oyediya, for the bond that serves as evidence of sameness of blood in our veins.

My beloved parents, Chief and Mrs. Nina Ndukwo Kalu Ugah, for their immense supports.

My editor, Kukogho Iruesiri Samson, for editing wisely, and my Granny, Mrs. Oyediya Obewu for my good upbringing and her belief in me to be a son in many sons.

My Uncle, Mr. Kalu Obewu and Mr. Michael Obewu, who always was a father, I appreciate their advice and encouragements.

Prof. Mkpa Agu Mkpa, Dr. Joe Emeson, Prince George Nnanna Kalu, Mr. Martins Agba, Prof. Uche Agomoh and Evang. Paul Nwokocha (The Gospel Governor). They are the pillars of character, emulation, and inspiration.

My lawyer friend, Linus Chibuike Ukpai Eni, and all the writers, poets, artisans, and fans of Arts, for your conviviality.

All my friends who understand, and to those that failed to understand, I thank you all.

COMMENTS

Ndukwo writes as though he resides in the mind of whoever reads his poems. In Orange Taste there is the picturesque expression of what is and what ought to be; simple yet deep poetry that speaks and interrogates and compels you to think and think and think again.

- **Ehi'zogie Iyeomoan**, writer, author of *Flames of the Forest (poems)*

In *Orange Taste*, Ndukwo versifies his thoughts on love, life, and politics as though conversing with the readers' consciences. His metaphors are original and refreshing.

- **Kukogho Iruesiri Samson**, publisher, photographer, author of *WHAT CAN WORDS DO* and *I SAID THESE WORDS*

Poetry as art forms challenges both the creative energy of the writer and the cognitive impulses of its readers.
Either way, it acts a supranational vehicle for echoing the human condition. As a genre of art, the beauty of poetry consists in its ability to distil the variegated canvass of humanity into recognizable nuggets for explaining who we are and why we do what we do.
Ugah's poetry explores the complexes of the human condition in Orange Taste. The poems in this book, crafted by Ndukwo Kalu Ugah and titled ORANGE TASTE, attempt to do just this. It treats wide themes ranging from racism, identity crisis to other existential concerns.
The poems, rendered in simple English, are easy enough to follow. Without any consistent structural patterns, the poems lucidly transport their reader into the heart of the subject.

In the Black Ant for instance, Ugah reflects on the fate of the pilgrim at the mercy of the elements and in what appears an unending battle with his identity. The individual is trapped between who thinks he is and the reality of his inability to be fully integrated into the mainstream of the society of adoption.

In all, Ugah's poem leaves the reader in a riot of emotions, causing him to reflect on his journey through life. They challenge him to engage himself and his society in a conversation, which hopefully, would birth a new society.
- **Nnamdi Okosieme**, journalist, Writer and Sports Editor at Timbuktu Media Limited

The "Orange Taste" as a collection of poems assures you more about creativity and insight. That had always involved an experience of acute pattern recognition, which the young poet Ndukwo Kalu Ugah uses in his compilation. It stresses straight to feelings, emotions and pierces into the marrow of the readers to foster and trigger the art-work in them.
- **Paul. I. Stanley**, author of *Information Technology and Society; Easy Approach & Practical*

Ndukwo Kalu Ugah

It seems that, out of the fruits I picked
Climbing the tree – long since felled
By the wind which had passed
And had had me down at last
Was the weariness for an *'Orange Taste'*

Orange Taste

Pictures in the frames

Pictures in the frames –
Our supposed grandparents
Gazing longingly on us
With no intent for a pause

These pictures are wall-mounted
Like one by the newly wedded
From their collection – shiny and awesome
I gaze at these pictures in admiration
Though old, they please like a purse of gold

I make sure the dust is not offensive
While rendering the services
But they hardly express any action

Sometimes, the wind blows them from a distance
And they display a dance
Commemorating their lives on the wall
Without a fall

These pictures tell a story
And are hanged to serve a memory
Of our grandparents
From what the images present

Strangers

Address others equally
In all languages
Share hospitality
To all strangers

It's the last supper
Cut out bread for dinner
And a piece of beef
Into equal sizes
To all strangers

Observe these exercises
Very frequently
And give the right ear
To all strangers

Gently comes a day
When, in deep problem
An answer will be given
As you gave, to all strangers

London Bridge

Invite the postmaster
And pay the charges for my letter
Written to my Beloved London bridge
Asking for her friendship

The bold, cemented carvings
Unveil mysteries
Which her contour shows
While sighting her at night

I'm in a special relationship
With the London Bridge
Holding her hands
On a walk to Africa
To be engaged and properly married

Who then shall compete
With the erection she gives
While she opens
For my lustful admiration?

The Prisons

Close the prisons
With or without reasons
And freedom becomes prisoners
Even reliefs to foreigners
Without guilt in Guantanamo

The magical king raises this signet
To reincarnate dead bones
And recipients of Stephens' stones
In pursuit of Golden Fleece
Towards national service

If you stay
The perpetuity of evil sprays
To the Afghanistan dump bin
Of sickly *Osama bin lan-din*
Losing his residence
To the king's presence

Now, cloud will gorge rain
If the king will heighten his reign
Thus a vision
With a summarized mission
That will end the existence of prisons
With or without reasons

Rats

Someday, in a country
Group of rats formed a choir
Like in a church in America

Roofs of many felt the presence of bombs
Like a touch by the Holy ghost
Beheading Toys found in fashion stores
With the noise of their concept of music –
Destruction!

They are smoked rats
Very black like Ghanaians
Riding on horses –
Voiceless
Yet they orchestrate the worst

These group of rats
Had formed a war squad
Like the Russian army
To take over the economy with ugly violence
Steering the quietness in our pots
These days
These rats increase in numbers
Competing with the Chinese
Inventing nothing but evil!

Know these rats!
Their cloths are red with torments
No river washes it without a stain
Know them when they come
For a call to white and green

Ndukwo Kalu Ugah

Freedom Throes

In fair dinkum
Biafra shall come!
Grow no dissension for freedom.
The chains in our hands shall earn us victory
Though in freedom throes
Yet leaving home to a no-father
Will always make dogs bark

Death rows particulate again in Biafra land
In a revolutionary margin
Eating heads and hearts alike
Whether killed or imprisoned
To cold, ambitious move
For a life …and to be free!

The sepulchral government
That has monsters at the head
Brought him for questioning
Then pounced on him

Study the Egyptian plaques
With glasses as sky-large
Beat your ears with hands, hammer-like
If you have no fears
The creator will let his people be free
In this time of great panic
Growing despair and anxiety

See, innocent Biafran babies are lifeless on the street
In the quest of freedom
Yet your mother births cruelty
And practices profanity

In fair dinkum
Biafra shall come!

How we became friends

I knocked open doors of fancies
To a voice calling through a hole.

On Monday we became friends –
Faint hopes enveloped me
In a vineyard devoid of grapes

On Tuesday, I wrote her letters
From a room with no windows
I found myself boiled up to degrees

She replied three times on Wednesday
Giving me such transports of joy
I was hitherto unable to imagine

On Thursday
While we were in gross darkness
We confessed a share in our emotions

I discovered what had surprised the world
On Friday – they said its love.
I was naturally apt to pay

I kissed her on Saturday
Where no witness was nearby
And I hope that I may be pardoned

To have unlocked the thoughts to love
And treat a woman with the utmost respect
While in prayers on Sunday

Love Me

I am yours, oh Adaku!
As bees to a honeycomb
You lure and mould me
With each lick

I have heard your voice
And, like a dog ensnared to
The whistling of its master –
It told of your love to me

You raise my hopes
With imputed feelings
To be the licking fire underneath
The cauldron of my heart

I skeptically rise
In the arms of faith
For your mouth only speaks love
And does spout in no deed
Come nearer, Oh Adaku!
In the sudden rush of emotions
With lips cobwebbed in love
And stay with me.
Draw me closer!
To the allure of the craving bed
Where we'll sink and float memories
Of you and I

Flies

There are flies in my eyes
And also in your eyes
They are cruel and wise.

These flies come with fire-light
Why do we have no right?
Homes, families are in the fight –
We all share the same plight!

These flies are agents of poverty
Depreciators of property slapping us cold-hot
Sneezing our hurt

I see these flies
Steadily safe keeping the files
And the polished certificates
Of a five-years-spent graduate

These flies are fatigues to intellectual achievement
unemployment – littering youths in the street
No, not even one has a fit!

These blood thirsty flies need spray
I must pray
Ask me not why –
They could kiss us!

Ndukwo Kalu Ugah

Let me cry

Let me cry!
From the smile last seen on her face –
　　amalgamation in the past
From the no alternative
Alarming her an Ibo

Tell me, according to specification
If you have no interest in girls
And no shines from the sun?
Or were you born to take no offer
But violence and condemnation?

Let me cry!
For she's gone with her beauty
Thus, her dress I knew only
On the morning-evening of her cold death
Leaving me with seized breath

Let me cry
And suffer high blood pressure!
I have lost a mother!
And a sister, a problem solver!
I now live hopelessly!
I am finished!

What is more?
What is worse?
Let me cry!

Orange Taste

Son, Father and Mother

When I was born
I plastered our home with salt
At least the flattery was gone
I brought the native joy home
Like visions in a dream
Now, the family has a long chin of laughter

> Burn the medicine pot
> Make no disagreeable mixture
> For my son is laid in the cot
> He is my image
> From the angels in human form
> A feature without deformity
> In him I see nothing but happiness

>> A baby arrives
>> It's my baby, our baby
>> Upon my milk, he survives
>> Safe from the hungers that may be
>> In his wanderings in between lands
>> His fate is in my hands

Father Around

Would you father
At the end of another month
Over your quest for a baby
Being already a cross of childlessness
Raising hopes in vain again?

Will meals still be prepared on time
Enabling an impression of sickness
As she publicizes her state
Of a purported pregnancy?

Must you father
Raising pressure on the abdomen
Of innocent children?

Would you tell me in confidence
The pains she feels
On her admission at the hospital –
Lying down semi-conscious
Like a wounded lion?

Don't you have an orbit of affection?
At least twice a fortnight
As she is not a cure
For the disease of barrenness

Sad Corner

My mind has been on a journey
Walking and walking farther
Thinking and thinking harder
Seeking the bracelet of life
That will guide my body
From poverty and its diseases
Isolation and darkness

Hopefully the end is here
To my sad corner
The mind has kept vigilant

Though no one journeyed alongside
The tight and darkest moments with me
There is all good to share with them

Drag me not again

Drag me not again
You old love
That wrestles me back into the mud
I'm weakly in amazement of your wonders
Father knows not his grandpa
Yet he wears you
And even extended the oldness to us

Drag me not again
In the harmattan of getting married
She knows you not
Keeping your plate of your goodness unwashed
Because her heart blues lust

Drag me not
I understand not
Why I'm your begotten
Whom you toss
And permit the world to tag me with foolishness
Because you live in me.

Better the world

Hatred and pretense
These are all I see
Doubting whose trust I should keep
Nobody, not even I
Knows the symbol of peace
That has love at ease

The morning sun births the day
Owing the evening its pay
Where every man shall die
And in the dust lie

I shall play the piano
And sing my best
Dancing the tunes of Africando
When good shall score the best

Then the candles shall spark
To the darkest of our lives
Outshining every bad on our tracks
For a change shall come diving

I care deeply
To give the world approval
When good scores the best completely
After all, we head out from the same oval

The world has grown strange
And we are close to the dust
Up and Down shall be our inheritance
I said all these in instance

Ndukwo Kalu Ugah

The crown of life

A crown of life shall be
To whosoever that believes like me
That Christ is Lord indeed
And Him alone has the lead

Men shall serve him
With songs and the seraph hymn
And His commands we all shall obey
To see His face on that glorious day

O, exalt Him with praise!
All nation, bless His name always
For He had called us unto a place
Actually a paradise, with His grace

A stroke, frees us from the touch of ills
Sea waves, He keeps still
He conquers all
Even death, nature and all!

My child, I shall tell His story
That He is the King of Glory,
Gethsemane, you shall not forget
Christ's agony and the bloody sweat!

Victory to victory, we shall run the race
To meet Him face to face
In my heart, His words are written
And I arise as He has risen

I Can't Stay

I can't stay –
Suspicions, too heavy
Spur me into regret
And dreams, no longer realizable
Kill my ambitions in heart!

You see through me
Never had much time for me
I needed it. You knew it
You needed it. I knew it

But where are the adhesives
To join heads in reasoning?
Unity, oneness, peace, tranquility…?

I can't stay –
For the days are short
The moon has gone
Darkness has come with
Slaps of sorrow
Tears and Mistrust

Your convictions are right
But my future is bright
Mine seems to you as pretension
(Or maybe it had the look of Lucifer?)

I have Jacob's sunrise
And no fruitless labor
Envy, you had harbored
But I needed to tell of tomorrow

Do not get amiss with me
Because, I just can't stay!

Rain In May

On your sneezes, farmers are bent to soar
Whenever the moon turns to a count of four
Regretting and rejoicing, we take you in

It rains in May, when the heaven frowns
And ties the weather in a log of clowns
The sign the rainbow makes
Makes us sad-happy, witnessing the rains in May

Mother buys an umbrella because of you
Surprisingly, I accepted it because of you
Fearful, when the thunder strikes
Ringing bells for the flies to chirp at night
And singing melodies of your might

Fast speeding May rains
Steer us to work with our brains
Sleeping will be so cool
Your advancement plugs a ripened planting season
Having mouth and hands in prison
Your stay is regretted
Though children enjoy your bath
Like a thought nursed by a bat

Now we know whenever the spider welcomes a fly
He will regret to have a try

Orange Taste

Save a mother

Save a mother
from an acid murder!

She erects me with her stone
sadly, from her birth zone…
I was effected from the fusing
and also affected with breathing

There was dark basement on the floor
Mother's blood passes not from its door

Joseph died after her!
Intentionally, from mother's mistakes after
The society negated childbirth from affected mother

Oh hear me, and save this fetus from acid murder!

Ndukwo Kalu Ugah

Together a country

Let the crisis grind to a halt
If even temporal
Now that we smile not happily
It will be all good news to the young
Tensions will be partially reduced
I will be glad if the country can have a cold lie

Like a young lad
That has no hurt in his feelings
You should not be offended by this suggestion
For the sake of my congregation
Whose mortal lives have ended
In no cordial atmosphere.

I thought the blood in our unity
Could form clouds, condense and rain
Lasting ages in our brain
Though violence ruins the duty
And factors of our success

In everyday – surely, tomorrow is unknown
All we have are not our own
And so we will pass away
In wait of Life's rewards

Streams of Love

Blind is love that sees in the dark
Gallivanting in ignorance
Whether rich or poor

Wicked is love that holds the brow cold
And slaps our presence with the silence of all we knew
Making us fools while in him

Lust is love that buys from the market
Of our now and the future – letting us be like vultures
In the Tree of Life that all perch on

Crime is love that gives us resounding blows
Amidst rough encounters
Yet we find an endless delight in time of its war

Greatest is love in mansions of affection
Adoring all flaws – keeping you as a child in me
Though the match is imperfect!

Brain Washed

In the fields of my armpit
They come again with bombs
    Priceless!
    Political !
    Personal!

Who do we have in the news?
    Sisters!
        Mothers!
            Brothers!
                Fathers
They are dead in those mild bombs
Rationally scattered like dog meat

Maiduguri!
    Sokoto!
        Jos !
They will be arrested
For making a telephone call that rings within seconds
It's a bomb!

We've been brainwashed
    Religiously!
    Politically!
Personally!

Squirrels drop bombs like nuts
Monkeys suffer the stench in the north
Humans eat strawberries
While enjoying the news
Truly, we've been brainwashed!

Orange Taste

What if we all went blind?

I.
Human minds inquire more
Why? Beauty all adore
In our world where no truth is faced

My eyes diffuse a quickening ray
When dead bodies are raised
Without cloth in mortuaries

I heave a sigh, how can it be?
That God, the Creator, masterfully made me
an image none can imitate

II.
Boldly, I approach my unnumbered foes
Because my livelihood is mine
And in good strength will I oppose…

But, what if we all went blind?
Beauty and ugliness, none would pay a mind
Nor acknowledge nature's night

And the rate at which the day pursues
When the morning shines its light
Dark and thick as blood

III.
O God! You emptied your image
Though none is measured to your age
Your love is infinite, and so free!

Can it be, that I should gain
A perfect life in me?
So free, and without pain?

IV.
Pitiful, we mortals die
Having said much truth and lies
In discerning both the wrong and right

If racism is vanquished
And we cannot tell between the black and white
We'll live happily indeed, like the rainbow

Orange Taste

A still place in the market

The joy of womanhood
AfiaNkwo, the only market that ever stood
In Abiriba, rewarding us so good
Here, your honour dwells

'Attention! Buy me!' has been the song of bells.
We are your folks, whom you feed
A bowl of food, you are indeed
Morning and night, we call for our daily needs
Though inflation and rain are all your pains
But your spirit of abundance remains

> *One day, my lips grew dumb*
> *Seeing a breeze that takes people without a ransom*
> *My chain falls to a ghost's casket*
> *Exposing the presence of immortals in the market*
> *Tainting sound, I hear*
> *Seeing ghost in white and clear*
> *The breeze turns and perseveres*
> *Up and down, goes waterproof and some baskets*
> *The ghost softly sings all day, "Let's play"*
> *Lo, it's a still place in the market!*

Really, it's a dream that I had someday
And I awoke on a bed so wet
Wondrous, it was a still place in the market!

Your life is in dust

Have my alcohol and a push
Imprisoned and tormented by a Kush
You wear madness' tag
On the street with your rag

> *Your steps are perfect and just*
> *But if worst attains the worst*
> *Your life is in dust!*

Have my blood and be rich
Imprisoned and tormented by a witch
You question the wisdom in decency
Now that life is so spiffy

> *Your steps are perfect and just*
> *But if worst attains the worst*
> *Your life is in dust!*

Have my anus and the fame
Imprisoned and tormented from its shame
Doubting the pleasures in the women's Mercury
You'll rot in the hands of a jury

> *Your steps are perfect and just*
> *But when worst attains the worst*
> *Your life is in dust!*

Orange Taste

Black Ant

A quest in every land
Accepting slavery without protest
You peep into the dinner table of your land
Inhabiting many a forest

The sun grazes you so black
While in search for food
In between life's race-track
Hunger has grimed you good

It rains often, thunders and you're not back yet
Your breed is scattered abroad
Catching the fishes with net
And the flies with fraud

You wear *agbada* in disguise of your identity
When the court sends lies of your reputation
And all are convinced – in human's brevity
You creep like a mouse at their insinuation:

Motionless but moving
Deafened and speechless
I told the bush burners to stop killing
But they chose to be restless

Happenstance beats its drums
Alarming of your homecoming
You intend smiling with crumbs
Though in dark and noon, you're always trading

Even while the land is hot
You stay to be victims of the burning bush
Now the church burns
And your dead soul runs

Hear me, black ants in the north
Possibly, you need a push!

Hail O Biafra

In the East rises the sun
In our veins runs the blood of the dead,
raped and enslaved

Sons of the soil, now strangers
are looking from the windows

The rising sun has now dimmed
yet we call and sing of our oneness
to serve our fatherlands

They breathe blood and war
destructions and hatred

Can we name the war?
Call it a name –
civil, intended, outbreaks?

It gives more heartbreaks
for a nation that is *sad-happy* to lay in pretension

We can't forget our roots –
The Promised Land.
Hail O Biafra!

Indeed, there was a country
out of the rebellion that I served

Without The Blacks

We are Africans, the blacks
The integral part of your existence
The origin of arts and innovations
Importers of your imaginations
Blessed are the blacks unborn!

Without The Blacks
Who buys your magic and witchcraft
How can you feed and get clothed?
Racism must be stoned to death!

Without The Blacks
Who could've appreciated
The sparks of your inventions?
Who will boost your economy
So you could feed and get clothed?
Their patronage did oil your mouth
Without The Blacks
Your fathers wouldn't have had a heaven on earth to explore

The gospel is untold and incomplete!
Racism must be stoned to death!

On The Feast Day

Babylon has been carried away
Beyond what is due, it wastes away
To the emergence of a Queen
Whom nations looked fairly upon

She isn't an eye to the roof
Unlike the ladies under our roof
She is lettered with favour
Eats not without the rest

Enough milk is in her breast,
The King annuls the laws of destruction
To hold her hand in the law of kindness
A sack-clothed uncle is now the next to the throne

All rivers run into her sea
To be a rescuer among nations
A banquet is set before the King
When the Jews cry bitterly

With her honour, love and humility for the king
He beats his chest in appraisal of her
On the feast day a banquet is set before the king
So that she could make a request

Who Dies Next?

Who dies next?

The news is next
Bent on causing terror
Some are calculated and assimilated in error
Skulls in the news will beg the question –
Why?

Children
Mothers
Fathers
They cry
She mourns
He dies...
In the maelstrom of ethnic hatreds

Who dies next from the virus that is now aberrant
With intense fear of the next victims?
The nature of my dreams is now lost!
Can we abjure the negative impacts in the news?

Ably we can arrest the ugly face
Affecting the entrails of our commune
Through a celestial intervention

In all these, I thank God

I thank God

Though the road was rough
In the chilly vehicle
I made an apologetic cough
I did call on God

On realizing of the bitter harshness before me
My stomach was uncomfortable
But my faith journeyed with me
Before my enemies, set is my table

The river bed was pale through the window
Within a word or two it was another morning
The chairs serve as my bed and pillow
In all these, I thank God

Held firm my respect
As I lay all day in his house
Though it had a tilted aspect
I have to lay like the mouse
Pride has been swallowed
Nativity, a thing of the past
In self-pity, I have wallowed
Now a week is my last

I got married to his trust
It is not surprising he did so badly
I stood all day, forgetful of self-lust
Personal, ideal but dangerous unknowingly
I have eaten sufferings with my teeth
Lamenting, I beckoned on God

In all these, I thank God.

Confined by the Night

The sun whirls by
The moon and stars
Long to see the world
Sparkle in the night

Lovers see the ill
And the devouring teeth of the night
Yet proceed in familiar
Habits in turning about
Making a vow and taking a bow
They either sit or stand about
In the large heart of the night

The blue sky has no light
Encrusted by its own effluvia
He has a demon to fight
As the darkness visits in my sight
And my weariness kept me awake in the fearful night

Tonight, every night
Has the golden right
To dispatch ears to the motherless' plight
Also he defends the widow in her fight
And the dying, he accelerates their might

Orange Taste

Negroes

Nature condemns us Negroes,
With marks of slavery beneath our toes

Our route was East-North-East
Driven by the wind at South-West
With only Africans aboard
The ships made better ways forward
In our utmost distress for food and water,
Africans grew all in good health, or strength rather

St. Peters' Church

Donation – a compass of their thought
A journey towards a God, they sought
I could simply differentiate the two
As the poor and strangers give too
Their common actions are with contempt
Describing it by circles or other geometrical terms
With observation towards political statements
And their lines of give-and-receive in parallelograms

Together Apart

Our love stole the moonlight
Accustomed by the festive night
Submitting us into silence
Painting the pictures of Adam and Eve

Fondling and kissing
Admiring and caressing

The breeze and trees paid minds to us
A rendezvous of our destinies
Inspiring each other with smiles
Written in bold letters

The ever blushing moon of our love
Faintly diminishes into the sky
Submitting us into regrets as we count the days
That we were brightened with the miracles of love

We now live under the skin of distance
Forgetting and forsaking the certainty
Of our feelings, emotions
And the heartfelt affections

Distance made us feel separation
Arresting the care for each other
We need changes
To buy back our closeness

Our Quest

We were on our own
And no mind was blown
Because the land was self-ruled
In the silent of the nights
We coughed out the fears
That rolled among us
We basked in the peace of our gods
Celebrated Christmas with the moon
Danced with open breasts and buttocks
Until they came:
The dark hearts in white descended like locusts
Ndi ogwumagala
The bees now beam in their best
Since then, Sim-sim-sim settles at the center
Tim-tim-tim is heard in the west
And Kom-kom-kom knows all the houses around
Gbuo gbuo gbu-o-o-o has hatched the eggs in its hands
Serenity bled
And the blood rolled over our ancestral lands
We have known many in a capsule
From their white flashing teeth
To their honey coated promises
We are no longer expecting quests
For our quests are behind our banana trees
The elephant that asked for shade took over the house
Let the gong of one Nigeria preach these messages
And treat these messages as razor
In a baby's hand

African Grasses

Herbs that heal
Grasses in the savannah
Africa is blessed with your miracles
And confident in your intimacy

When ailments grip me with cold hands
You stand in defense for me
And sacrifice much to make me live

Your power can't be measured
Nor compared with Whiteman's drugs

The beauties of Africa
With power to heal
In fearful nights of *tams* and *kpoms*

You are on the mountains
And also on the hills

Oh! African grasses!
Though the farmers set out to kill you
Your maker made you stand still
Blushing with boundless greenness

Oh! African grasses!
What are *Irokos* if not you?
Africans are blessed with you!

Tamer of all

Body deteriorates at your coming
Your victims you tame
None has ever loved you
None has ever invited you
You saunter where demons fear to tread
You cannot be stitched with threads
For you're as big as Mount Everest
None can have you and rest!

Your slaps are resounding,
Old and young go crying, reeling
Under your intense power
You have no mercy
Not for the arrogant nor the lowly
Your strikes are surgical
Giant goes weak at your touch

I would walk miles to know you
But you won't show yourself
As I feel you in stomach, head, tooth...
Friendly, you are not
Let's be together, you cannot
I wonder why you were created
Why were you made?
A terror in aerated bodies

Scientists fight but conquer not
They try to apprehend you
Using pills in many names
But they can't, never
Because you are a die-hard beast
Small as a mosquito
Stinging like bee
Vicious as the tornado

Orange Taste

You are a bed of thorns
Ironed with names and description
You travel far and wide
A terror to a black and white
You are guilty of genocide
So you ought to rot in jail.

Shall I live or die?

Speedily, he grows
Gaining shoulders and muscles
He adds faster and faster
In bodily forms

His life meets the fence
And the accidental motions
Of the Earth and Sun
Leaving him to the eclipse of life

As the time goes by he becomes his universal artist

He draws himself to alcoholism
Late nights, women and cultism
He dislodges himself from education.
Between the numbers of verbs and nouns,

Mother!
Who is my father?
Why was I cursed?
Shall I live or die?

A boy of peace

Who can save him that was deprived
of love of a sweet mother who passed at midnight
while birthing him?

What shall become of him that limps
and is afflicted with pus
for being deprived of breast milk?

Who shall touch him that lays with skin disease
down on the floor, paralyzed by NAB injections
in attempts for a cure?

A boy of peace grows, aiding his movement with stick
He builds his own world, art crafting with hands
despite his deformity

He finds a better him
in the interpretation of his dream and in the truth
that God cares and makes possible his daily bread

Public Funds

Solve the mathematical figure
And tell of the amounts in your seizure
To tell the most iniquitous
Favoring fraud and oppressions among us

Can the truth take us backwards?
And falsehood in the near forwards?
Their offices is a convenience to fund carriage
Wholly political appointments, an advantage

How can I mind my cow
While injustice takes up a bow
In prodigious speed
To injure and make the nation bleed?

Imagination can figure nothing
Whether they were milked at home or abroad
Being confounded with the essence of everything
As they thought, nature picks them with a nod

They have tempered laws
Occasioned civil wars
In description of bullets
Bombardments and muskets

The nation floods tears
And lives in fears
It is maxim among these politicians
That biases their lives against equity

Poor nations become proud
Crusading our faults aloud
Tagged us the rich but hungry
Thus a bird of prey, for its cruelty

Orange Taste

To this nation
All the rest of the people are slaves
For the law has no expression
To bid these diversions with waves

A poet's mind

A poet's mind
Forms a cloud to the blind
There, he has rain and sunshine
Fastened to many reasons
With a sensible touch by these seasons

He writes through windows
Till the yellow sun arises
Standing so long with heads erect
He dishes his silver words in sizes
Baked and served in their slices

He chiefly dares
What could cause the nature of arts
Attractive and universally reckoned
Between the bowels of the earth
He knows when the sun is late
To exhale water and gorge rain
Pointing downwards and upwards
With circumstance of wonders inwards

Mother-In law

Yesterday, past gone
Were the years we made love –
There was no conveyance of hate
Shouts and arguments

We were the 'connoisseur artists'
Watched freely at the cinema hall
By neighbors and passers-by on the street

Events took us together
And we became Adam and Eve
Naked in the heart with clothes of sincerity

When we invited mother over
To stay and share the warmth in the furnace of our love
The days turned grey in colour

I could remember
They shone like friction over stone
And ignited a difference in our union

Mother became a bone
She made us cat and dog with figurative rants
She seldom cooked meals that had not my share
Of the tortoise and the elephant stories

I mourned with a pregnancy –
Each night from her kicks in quest for a child
I prayed

Deliverance came sooner
And healed our wounded love
That turned the marriage we cherished into rusted metal

My Child

My child!
Always put on your smiles
And ensure you fly in miles
Deservedly, you will be admired
Even after youthfulness has expired

My child!
Do not give Pride a seat
He will kick your feet,
To a horrible fall –
A push to the wall

My child!
Offer Arrogance a slap
And Blessing will wear you a cap
Allow Patience to hear
Your stories with the right ear

My child!
Shun idleness
And make hard work a business
It holds your greatness
While in your world of littleness

Orange Taste

Father

A man of wide culture
        you stand and sit in good posture

In describing your virtues seen
        we saw nothing, not even sin

Though mankind is merely cruel and dirty
        Your good on men are rated enormously

Forgiveness is within the jug of your heart
        where mercy could be sung to a rat

Some had died but others live
        and your kind never leaves

Your shines emerge like the sun
        amidst skies painted in crimson

A reasonable being in a world of fools
        where nothing good rules

You had lived to die, but when
        till our grandchildren are men?

We may copy your description
        but cannot be you in true proportion

For you wear garments of glass
        and drink air squeezed into bras

A trip in *gwongworo*

The truck horned with a call upon a market day
In the next town, to pick all traders
But they out-did the noisy calling
In making preparations while others ate

The men climbed perfectly
Likewise the women – each with a knot on her abdomen
They alighted, opening their legs
Viewed freely by any who cared

I chiefly held my observations:
Their breasts fluttered
As their buttocks also swaggered
And kept men in never-ending tensions
For their eyes shone like the moon
Continuously, like the sun at noon

After an hour's riding
Upon the free air, dust and sunshine
I overheard the shouting
From the *agberos*, for the driver to pay dues
Oya! oga move
And the driver geared and drove off

The passengers, shouting, yelling, and laughing
At the same time, to wholly overcome fears
Commotion, the long standing
And the inanimate sounds that fed our ears
Pot-holes and gallops became the headache of many

"Please driver, take it easy!"

Orange Taste

Let's call back

The eagle is now blind
Much unlike an owl in pitch darkness
The Benue and Niger have become tides that nurse sadness

Let's call back the brain
Toiling and working, not in vain
Let's call home and keep vigilance
Let the old wisdom be given a chance
Through agriculture, that we may gather gold
Now that the oil-economy grows old

The economy crumbles under confusion
While the masses lives in pain
Under the weight of mass acquisition
Being fitted to *old-new* change again
Knots and spanners tighten no more
While eyeballs drop to the floor

Let's call home quickly
Let's wear the old heart a new dress
The old costumes fit perfectly
And minds work with no stress
For religion has erected illusive altars in people…

Politics waltzes in welfare
Raising appetites in any penny that comes by
In denial of the monthly share
That bids a good bye
In the mouth and hands of the civil servants
Lastly, to the domestic life of ants

Ndukwo Kalu Ugah

An Igbo

In the course of creation
I became an Igbo
Owing father and mother an obligation
And treating them as so

To fulfill these
I met with friends, privately
Who are also in search of geese
A German kind, outside our country

*'Arrest him, arrest him
He is a criminal!'*
I considerably sang my last hymn
Sweating blood, for today is my final

Who will tell my story
And give such account of me?
I lamented my own folly to God
The only savior that be

Orange Taste

Come back brother

I sit here staring at the past
When you loved me
And desired not to betray
The sound of brotherhood
That beats steadily in our hearts
Da dum da da dum

Slowly, we danced
And made joyful expressions
From the steady sound at rooftops
The sound of brotherhood
Da titi da titi
It beats ever more

Come back brother!
Now the sound is long gone to moments of grief
When our wears, the coat of chameleons
Brought bad habits to infest
And hidden jealousy incubating in us

We have grown slowly apart
Our hearts, burdened with clouds
And that which I could see I now can see no more
We thirst from our palms
Before, in them water abounds

Come back, brother!
I have called back the dogs
And the bees on the fly
To tame your breath
For you no longer owe me any bone
Though you do – I will never ask.

I dream to see you in the beauty of the rainbows
The simplicity of nature and the brightness of the world

God will give us peaceful sounds
To dance again

Scriptures must be fulfilled

I knew nothing, Pilate
When you gave me to crucify
In the silence of the world
No one said good of me
Though I taught them in the temple

All mocked me
Lay abuses and spat on me
Parted with my clothes
And gave sour wine
While I thirsted

But go your way
And tell the scribes
That I had destroyed the temple
Likewise built another
In three days.

Also tell the scribes
Though I died with the transgressors
On earth, I resurrected
And live with the creator
As the king and Saviour to them

Tell them that I be not far
My presence stays with the world
In the lips of my disciples
For here and there, goes my word.

The tree of life

Keep awake, brothers and fall not asleep
For our boat is taken by the waves of the troubled sea.
While you sleep, our blood, will be spilled
To the fishes and the crocodiles
Whose golden land we invade

Hold not unto the breeze that lures you to sleep
Now that we've lost our trace
And you shall never find me again, brother
While in your deep dreams
Sailing unto death

The winds come to us with no shoes
And give us to death
Unto a land that knows not our birth
That beholds our grave in the bellies of daring fishes
Crowded to the sides of our boat

They not have done us any injury
While the malicious moon watches
The time and the day when we go abroad
To the solemn land
Of the dead

There, we'll struggle with him and the tree
The tree of life that saves
Only if we could watch and pray!

Orange Taste

The craftsman

Who can compare the artisan that transforms
Our landscapes, armed with varied skills
To a trader that only buys and sells
Depending on whatsoever nature gives?

Shall we then measure the craftsman
That is skilled with bare hands – dexterous in his craft
To a businessman who knows only numbers in currencies
And suffers loss, if exchange should slap?

Note me well
The artisan lends his hands to the building of great cities
From the pristine state to the modern
They made Rome, Paris and London…

Why should we put Aristotles in positions of importance?
For they only propounded philosophies.
Between the pipe and the theory
Which holds waters better?

Ndukwo Kalu Ugah

A walk in alcohol

He moves under the influence of distilled spirit
With no foot to trace
The bones and all between his teeth
Preserve the liquor, on his face

Don't scold him, let's call his wife
Open your eyes and save your life
Many are here, that stand at ease
Waiting for your age to have a cease

You ring drunk in the town
And make good for a clown
The bottles, the glass cups need a check
To shake off the alcohols in your neck

You have fallen, infallibly
To the floor, shamefully
*'Hold him, hold the legs to the ground
And save him from the rebound'*

Orange Taste

War danced

The land is flooded in happiness
For the men are returning
From the war that fed up their calmness
And had had the kingdom slackened

As they advanced forward
Many began raving over their heads
Their hearts pumped harder
Expressing joy, upon unexpected hopes
To win a war, each came out with the daughter
The wives embraced needle-tears in ropes

The gates saluted their returns
In open arms, clutching their rifles
The vultures also took their turns
With a constant look at the nipples

The war is danced
When the bravest wins
Honour and lives are restored
And the knowledge of resolution begins

Child Loss

There, where the people in white
Work frantically
We wait

We are in open expectation
To herald your arrival
As we wait

Our hearts clocked in high pulsation
The spotless face and your first smile
We wait

There where babies cry relentlessly
And the mind is trapped in the midwife's thoughts
We wait and make you wishes

We are in fast rehearsal
For gibbering
There where she lies in labour pains

As the kicks grow in endless pains
Clutching her senses
We felt a birth that was to be

It seems the time has turned backwards
As the gadgets finds their way
Into your nostrils and the mouth

Forcing the fleeting life back
As your screams become faint
There we wait

Orange Taste

Wedding day

Henceforth, you shall not steal
Again from the pot of the married
Porridge cooked in the spirit of the heavenly
To be eaten and shared privately

While single, you thought not for the sweetness
In the meal, only seeing it as a mystery
A boiling pot of doom with bitterness to life

Today is a happy day that envisages
The beautiful life ahead
And the future full of happiness
Where you will share embraces and sweet romance

A union with lots of adventures
With the *I do and I do* that starts with kisses
Over the ring on your fingers

Ndukwo Kalu Ugah

Okomba

Agbala kaa ni!
Agbala kaa ni w-o-o-o
My corpse greets the land.
Agbala ekelelam unu w-o-o-o

Greetings to *Okomba* family
Their son, who traveled to Amerika
Long years ago by the aid of his kinsmen
Is back home
Dead!

Invite the village crier
Let him announce my arrival
And instruct the village to gather;
Let them mourn my birth
And rejoice over my death

Tell my mother
That I slept on the laps of Amerika
Milked her breast
Felt the warmth of her forbidden
And forgot the greetings in our land

Call the men
Seated in their bamboo bed
Let them gather too
Dish out kola nuts and pots of wine
Let them eat, drink
And regret my birth

Let the native chalk
Write me on the blackboard
And teach Afrikans about me
About the heritage of her sons
On an extensive trip

Orange Taste

Inform my Amerikan wives
That my shoes bear my foot mark
And my children shall return as I did
Once they smell the sweet savor of Afrika

Let them return home alive
With two cocks in their hands
Okomba, will not be stolen from my waist
They shall be welcomed from song to song
The song of Afrika!

Chinua Achebe

Though you are without breath
You live as your writings
There lies a river
Flowing with ink, blood

To an endless race…yours has ended
A river entrenched in the academe
I saw the ruination, gangrene
That had you rejected
From a long -built emotional quotient

Your literary uniqueness gambols
The good-evil, has taken you
To have you is a better-good dill
River Lake adjoins you and I
Thanks to Heavens!

Mosquitoes

>Arise, lifeless body
>and feed me more
>as the day goes greedy
>to steal from your shore…

Mosquito, leave me alone
and drag not my feet
to your fearless throne
where you make blood meat
For when I die
I'll be buried in your piteous eye

>Advice the gutter that it shines
>and springs not with dirt
>Your backyard is a guilty shrine
>in what charge, if not malaria and death?
>If I disturb you not while sleeping
>then know that cleanliness is worth keeping…

I will be alright
though I lay like a log
awaiting your commanding might
while asleep like a watch dog
once I clap, you will die
and lifeless, you shall lie…

>Though little I be
>and winds blow me away with a whisper
>I appreciate nature that made me
>an irritation in all your day
>Advice homes on clean-up exercises…

>For we're many in bigger sizes!

The Youth

The heart pumps her curves as tempting
Energizing the blood to beat the drum

As she walks, focus makes a home between her thighs
Eventually, the mouth knows nothing
What could speak now
but the strokes penetrating in and out?
The knee begs a stop
yet the waist grows angrier

Who chews the pregnancy in your belly?

The palm cries in heavy heats
While her father slaps to know
Emphasizing that kola sweetens
But sugar never bitters

Bent on what the nose sees
the ear perceives
the negativity of what the eyes hear
and lets the head be the culprit
which death nurses

The media bags the complain
to have killed the future
in giving rise to rape
playing abnormally with dangers
in all, the youth are the most vulnerable!

The new God

We found a new God
Who runs in another blood
Clear as tunnels in his veins
And limps as planes
In his wandering flight
Without stars for sight

In his morning he rises from the eye of the sun
And hardly births fun
From the wave of his evening
Through the cold night
That claws his flight

A new God?
Some say, in their oddness
That he lives in the West – a sanctuary of forest spirits
Far off the East, where humans would never go for a feast

Is Pythagoras, the God?
In motion of his backward and forward
Fetching laws to his favour
Smells anus for the odour
Conspired of air and water for earth
Thus strangling humans' breath

He dehydrated our cry like rain
And felt the new world in pain
By setting his mat across the sea
In his sleeps for the kingdom's key

Yet died with Abraham's greatness
Without Lazarus and his wellness

Ndukwo Kalu Ugah

They clap death

They clap death, the war conformists
Whom had gonged their heart to kill
Giving rise to social pathologies
Planted in the tree of memory

They clap war, the charlatan warriors
Calling distance examples of war scenes
Masterful in bloodshed
Repudiating the continual confluence in the Niger

I sense the selection of the corruptible
Intensifying havoc in our lives
With shortened, substantive hope for peace and security
Because of these religious sect fearing no god or man

Tranquility has gone on an extensive trip
To return with the freedom of the people of the rising sun
A country that once existed
A conflagration of the corruptible

Our men are broken
Blanched by the actions of the killing buckets
Disunity is the bread we feed upon
And we have grown to stay with its taste

They dance war and have grazed with its mark
But peace must go in great guns in Nigeria

Orange Taste

Ojukwu

Ojukwu, oh my Ojukwu!
The eyes that greets the world of Biafra
Neck and neck
You did fight for Biafra
You've had the finality our sojourn
Bathed with my threnody

You need not our tears
For you've had the score cards of ethereal

Odumegwu, oh my Ojukwu!
The candle of our light
You've held love in good faith
For the Hebrews – the Igbos
You did whet their dreams.

You had dealt with political skullduggery
In pursuit of harmony that has an axe to grind

Ikemba, oh my Ikemba!
By your touch, souls were united in love
Tyranny transformed and we balanced hopes
You served your people at the helm,..

I am indebted
As a teeny-bopper summiting in silence
To the corridors of your bravery
Your scheming for the Igbos

I and the Igbos will
Albeit the presence of insinuations
Celebrate your memory

Ndukwo Kalu Ugah

Tragedienne

I am Fesse
A girl of twenty
I will now cry
For I read books with no gills
Yet come good with passes
In trade with bodily exposures

Now hands are dry
And the scorch of the sun
Makes much kills
While I stand with men in clean-cut
That makes hearts go for chariots

I had thrown into pit
The *"you are of pure-bred*
And should have a hair-cut"
That was preached on the pulpit.

'Think Twice' I did say
It's an advice
And never a gainsay

My ways are now drawn in a graph
For I bend on beauty, shapes and curves
In the tonality of the coins they bring
HIV sensed…

My habitual steps
Grow so serious
Likewise, life turns censorious.

'Think twice' I did say
It's an advice

Orange taste

What is poetry?

Sublimity –
     a pillar in the castle
          of literary arts

What is poetry?

Realities
     oxygenated
          with words

What is poetry?

Protector of tenets
     upholding humanity
          and her values

What is poetry?

Stipulation of emotions
     hopes
          and aspirations

What is poetry?

An orange taste –
     condensed, revitalizing
          sweet!

Ndukwo Kalu Ugah

Orange Taste

www.ingramcontent.com/pod-product-compliance
Lightning Source LLC
Chambersburg PA
CBHW051349040426
42453CB00007B/479